COVERT ABDUCTIONS

Military Harassment, Surveillance, Interrogation & Mind Control

AUTOBIOGRAPHY OF A SURVIVOR

Volume 1

MIESHA JOHNSTON

DEDICATION

I dedicate this book to all the women and men who are suffering in silence, isolated and in fear of what happened to them, and feeling like they could be losing their minds because of the memories that are surfacing for them. I too felt like this couldn't really have happened to me, until I delved more deeply into it. I hope that some information found in my book will encourage you to share your experiences in a safe support group or maybe inspire you to even write your own book.

TABLE OF CONTENTS

ACKNOWLEDGMENTS

I want to thank the people who made this book possible:

Authors Janet and Sasha Lessin for all the help and encouragement.

Emmeliesa for proofreading and editing this current edition of the book.

Joanna Summerscales for her help in editing the first edition of this book.

Mary Munoz and Hanna Messoline for their support and help. They are also writing a book about their experiences.

Steve Wachholtz for his cover illustration.

Artists Christine Dennett and David Chace for providing illustrations for this book.

MILAB ABDUCTIONS AND THE THREAT

I write this book to let you know that, no matter what you have gone through in your life, you can change your perspective to make it a positive, happy experience. What I call Love and Light. I want to help others who have gone through similar things, to let them know that they are not alone, not crazy, and they don't have to be victims.

I started my groups in 1991 for women, men, teens and children who are contactees and experiencers (abductees) of ETs, to provide a safe place for others to share their experiences. I started the first teen and children's groups in the United States in 1994. I was also the director of U.F.O.C.C.I. (UFO Contact Center International) and Celestial Contacts of Nevada, and was a working group member of Steven Greer's C.S.E.T.I. in Las Vegas.

In my groups we discuss our positive and negative experiences and whether they involved contact or abduction. I provide a place for people to share their real stories; the stories about their own experiences, whether terrible or good. They have a safe place to share their heart, their soul and their emotions about what happened. These groups are a place for people to give support to each other, absolutely knowing what each other has gone through and knowing what it's like to live such a life. They have an opportunity to share everything, all the details about their experiences, and we talk about all facets of what contact and abduction phenomenon involves. As people share their experience it helps others who have gone through similar experiences to understand their own, and it allows a person to not feel so alone, in both their experiences and in their lives.

There are many kinds of experiences. I will name a few, beginning with the positive: ET contact, CE3 (sightings), CE4 (contact), CE5 (conscious contact, either angelic or with ascended masters). Some negative experiences include: MILAB (military lab abduction, or military re-abduction), alien abductions, or MK-Ultra (mind control). The following projects are under the umbrella of MK-Ultra: Project Monarch (sex slavery and ritual abuse), Project Montauk (slaves used for time travel and experiments), Project Disney (child trafficking), Project Talent (information couriers, drug couriers, psychics, remote viewers), Project Artichoke, SSP Secret Space Program and Super Soldier Program (time travel, spies, and super soldiers: where they kidnap children, teens, men and women to work on other planets and other timelines and dimensions as basically slaves and sometimes soldiers, if they're lucky). There are also remote programs where people become targeted individuals (who experience psychotronic torture, voice-to-scull, nano technology and microwave torture). There's lots more information on YouTube and the internet that you can listen to and read about this. I suggest that everyone reads up on these subjects. It's all true, not to mention their new programs that we know nothing about. If you've seen it in the movies, they have it.

It is important to go through the memories that you do have. We need to clear the fear, anger and hate because people and the planet are going through an ascension and we must be ready, or we will get left to stay in this matrix that we're living in now.

I also don't wish to incarnate back into this matrix prison planet. I am writing this book to explain my own experiences, and I hope that as you read my book it might help you understand your own. These are my experiences as I remember them.

I believe that most of my ET experiences have been of a positive and spiritual nature. I will write about some of the positive and some of the negative things that have happened to me in my life, but I am not a victim, and neither am I the result of these things that happened to me. I am who I am because of the things that I have experienced in my life, whether they were good or bad. They have made me a more non-judgmental, understanding and loving human being, which is an important quality for the groups I facilitate and the people I counsel.

I have been aware of the elite and military

involvement in my own contact off and on throughout most of my life. I do not know who exactly these groups are and who has abducted me but I believe it to be a small faction within our military and shadow government. I have had several abductions which began with an alien, only to end up in the hands of the military, or to be dropped off by ETs and then find myself being picked up by the military on the same night or a day or two later.

I would also wake up in odd places such as in the back of a van, a ranger type jeep or a black helicopter (the experiences with the latter have resulted in a phobia and now I hate to fly). I would then be taken to a joint military/alien facility or base. I have memories of going down in elevators to floors where military and aliens seem to be working together.

I have many recollections of being taken into a small room with gray walls and being interrogated, sometimes treated abusively. I have woken up with bruises all over my body, including my arms, inner thighs, ankles, wrist, and even my stomach. My interrogators have been men in uniform, people in white smocks, and reptilian aliens. (By the way, body scars will show up better under black light that is the same black light as used in night clubs.)

During an experience once I learned more about another kind of reptilian, which I saw in the DUMBS. One night I went to bed in my home and woke up walking down a hallway with gray polished rock walls. There was a smell of damp and sickening sulfur, which could have been coming from the large reptilian creature that I was walking next to. I didn't know how this was happening and now think it had to have been drugs. Since I was walking on my own but I was under some kind of control, maybe I was under the alien's control? I could not turn my head or move my eyes from side to side, and I could only walk forward. I was scared out of my mind but could not scream, cry or run, which I wanted so badly to do.

As we walked down the hall I saw men in black uniforms, most of them carrying guns, walking the opposite way towards me. Every time we passed they would look me up and down like I was a piece of meat, since I was an attractive young woman. I hated that. The strange thing was that even though they would leer at me they never looked at the reptilian. I knew he was walking next to me. I thought to myself, "Now, why don't they look at him?" A strong powerful voice came in my head and said, "They know better, they must honor us." I can understand that because the reptilian was very menacing looking. He had been communicating with me through telepathy, which I feel is one of the reasons that I was abducted, because I could understand the messages he was thinking and sending. I got the distinct feeling that there were not many of us that could telepathically speak with them.

Their messages also include imagery so I actually saw some soldiers get in dangerous trouble by looking at him or any other ones in his rank. I continued with the walk down this musty smelling hallway, wondering what in the world was waiting for me at the end since I was being escorted by a reptilian. I thought, "Why are you invading our planet? What do you want with our planet?" Again I heard the powerful voice in my mind, "We are not the invaders, you are. We were here first!" In these communications I was also shown pictures of what he was saying to me. I saw imagery of raptor-like dinosaurs during an extinction event. Some of the more intelligent species such as the raptors went underground and survived, which would mean they were here before us. From that point on I had looked at reptilians differently.

The reptilians such as the raptors went underground millions and millions of years ago, and by the natural evolution the reptoid species have evolved to who they are today. Races such as the Draconian race are probably the most misunderstood. I witnessed a deep respect for this race from many planetary systems, generated out of admiration and fear. The Draconians are the oldest reptilian race in our universe. Their forefathers, somewhere in our most ancient past, came to our universe from another separate universe or reality. When this actually occurred no one really knows. Draconians themselves are unclear how or when they came into this universe but what is interesting is that they declare and teach to their masses that their species was here in the universe and on this planet first, before human beings, and that they are the true heirs to the universe and as such are all royalty. Therefore they are brainwashed at a young age, just like we humans have done to our younger generations, that they are above all as the royalty of all humanoid races in the galaxy. The Draconian race is composed of master geneticists who tinker with life, which from their perspective exists as a natural resource.

The Draconians look at life and see what they have created or altered. They feel that they had something to do with the primate race which had been modified 22 times. This primate race eventually became Homo sapiens, the race of our human bodies.

THE RITUAL & HOSPITAL STAY

My first memory of being taken into a DUMB (Deep Under Ground Base) was at age 16 in Arco Idaho, 1965. I remember going to bed one night, and my next recollection is that I was aware of a woman with almost white skin and dark black hair with a widow's peak, who was wearing white. I thought she was a nurse.

My next recollection is of standing in a field with a very large whirring sound above me, and when I looked up I saw a very large object (ship) above me. I could see moving parts on the bottom of the ship, like individual turning wheels all rotating in different directions, both clockwise and counter clockwise. I sensed someone or something standing behind me. At that point the nurse literally handed me over and then disappeared, so I'm thinking she really wasn't a nurse at all and perhaps she was a reptilian who had shapeshifted or made me see her as a human woman.

There in the field were two tall Draconian reptilians. They wore long dark robes so it was hard to really see them. What I could see is they were at least 7 ft tall with dark green scaly skin. I was able to see them later in the underground base, and I remember their skin felt like alligator scales. They also had piercing red and yellow eyes, a ridge that went up their foreheads, and they had a snout and a lot of teeth.

The memories I have are of being underground as part of a sexual project. They told me I was specially chosen and part of a special race and bloodline, and they told me they owned me.

I experienced a horrible ritual. I was surrounded by the cloaked reptilians and I was given something that caused extreme sexual arousal. I heard some languages I didn't understand, and they were chanting words like "Abendia". Some other names came up too. I was wearing a white robe as I felt like I was representing a priestess. There is no other way to say this, so I will go ahead, hard as it is to share what I recall of what happened to me. Here is where it gets hard to remember and separate the different times this has happened to me in my life. When you have had as much missing time in your life as I have, all time runs together and I find it hard to remember things in chronological order. I remember there were men and aliens. There was ritual with rape and victimization. I also remembered other young women laid out on an alter with fire all around us. There were some who were sacrificed to the reptilians, who sucked up our fear adrenalin as if it was a drug or nourishment for them. The energy equated with this was ritual abuse. I felt high. I was told that I was a priestess. I found myself chanting words. My mind went blank and I lost consciousness. I found myself waking up outside my house. Was it a horrible dream, I wondered, or perhaps a memory from another life? Either way it was a terrifying experience.

We have been led to believe that our day to day life is the only true reality, but with metaphysical teaching you come to know that is not true. Actually, your day to day so-called 'real life' is the dream. I believe that we are multi-dimensional souls living a human life, and that we live other lives simultaneously. I believe that many of our dreams are realities that are happening to us on another timeline of Earth.

I have taken a few details out of this chapter, such as names, dates and places, to appease those in power. Just four days ago I was right to the day to publish my book, and I had sent it in once for editing and had to resend it because of some formatting problems. That morning at 6:00am January 4, 2017 I was hit with what I think was a psychotronic weapon that hit my pancreas and caused me excruciating pain to my abdomen. Through these waves of pain I was able to turn off my Wi-Fi but that didn't seem to help. The damage was already done. Through the almost unbearable pain I called two of my targeted friends who were remote viewers. They got a clear reason for why the attack happened and they could see who was doing the attack. My first pancreatic attack happened two years from when I first starting writing my book. I know this to be true and I know they are trying to stop me from writing this book. For this reason I must get it out. I am laying in a hospital bed on January 7, 2017 finishing this last chapter.

PSYCHOTRONIC HEART ATTACK

In June of 1999 I was abducted in Sedona while visiting with my friend, Heidi. I had gone to bed that night and was taken/abducted to Boynton Canyon, which is well known in Sedona for being a DUMB entrance. I was taken in a van with other people they picked up along the way. The men who took me wore dark colored uniforms. We were taken inside the mountain to a laboratory where I was put into coveralls and taken into a hazmat area (clean area). There were humans in hazmat suits who put electrode wires on my head, which sent electrical impulses to my brain. I remember seeing tall insectoid aliens, I believe in the clean room.

While I was gone from my friend's house my friends had woken up and had been looking outside to see where I'd gone. When they couldn't find me, they decided I must have taken a walk and they went back to bed. The next memory I have is of waking up the next morning, and my friends asking me if I had gone on a walk in the night. I said, "No, I don't think so. I just remember a very weird dream," and I told them about the experience I had in the DUMB. I did have more of an understanding as to why they took me in the first place, which became clear to me on my way back home.

I was in the car, on the passenger side, driving home with three other friends when I received some kind of a message. I was getting psychic impressions of a very strange image of a pod, and it certainly felt like a reptilian pod. The vision I got was of an egg shaped dark brown pod with a human/reptilian hybrid contained in it against his will. At the same time, I was getting a message telepathically from someone who was saying, "Please help us, please help us." I got the strong impression it was a hybrid child of a light green color perhaps, and that it was the being in the pod.

All of a sudden I started having chest pains which made me think I was having a heart attack, and I began hyperventilating and couldn't get my breath. I was really worried about what was happening to me. The driver of the car pulled over, the girls got a pillow and a sleeping bag out of the car and set it up against the back wheel of the car where I sat down, and they instructed me to take deep breaths, but I was still feeling the pain and could not get my breath.

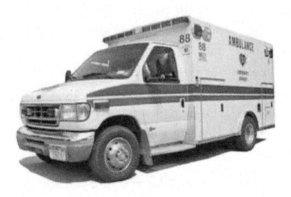

Strangely, just then, an emergency vehicle pulled up behind the car where I was seated on the ground. We didn't have time to have made a 911 call when it pulled up. Two men got out, one wearing a white shirt and white pants and one wearing a white smock jacket and camo fatigue pants underneath. He was also wearing military issue black boots. When I saw them I was quite frightened because I knew something didn't feel right. The other girls mentioned that it didn't look like the usual paramedic truck either.

They approached our vehicle but stood about 10 feet away from the car.

I believe this event was related to the vision that I had had in the car, just prior to the attack. The two men said, "She looks like she's having a heart attack. We need to get her inside and put her on our Defib machine." I told the girls, "I'm really afraid that if I go in that van you'll never see me again."

They brought no EKG, defibrillator or any other equipment from their van. It is my understanding that paramedics and emergency vehicles always have resuscitation and emergency equipment or testing equipment so for this reason, alarm bells were ringing. We were sure they were not who they said they were and I declined to be taken in their truck. I told them I thought I was just experiencing a little heat stroke, and said that I'd be fine.

They asked again, "Are you sure you don't want us

to check you out?" They said to my friends, "We need to get her inside so we can check her out and see what's going on with her." I whispered again to my friend, "No, don't let them take me." I said to them, "No thank you, I'm fine." They went on, "Well, if you don't come with us and something happens to you it's your responsibility. This is your last chance." Once again I said "No, I think it's just a little heat stroke, I will be fine. I'll just rest here."

Right about that time a sheriff's car pulled up at the front of our car, and before the sheriff could exit the vehicle the two men were back in the van and had gone. The pain that I was feeling began easing up and I was feeling better by the time the sheriff walked up to me. He said, "Are you okay? Everything all right here?" I said, and my friends backed me up, that I just got a little too much heat and needed some fresh air. The sheriff said "Okay that's good, I just wanted to check on you," and got in his car and drove off. It was very strange that the pain stopped right about the time the van left us. I felt that they were directing some kind of psychotronic frequency at me.

I have been facilitating experiencer support groups since 1991 for people who are MK-Ultra and targeted individuals. I have had many people talk about how they felt when they were under attack, having chest pains and a heart attack caused by some kind of frequency that was aimed at them. What we found out is that the frequency they shoot at us causes symptoms of a heart attack, but it is not a heart attack. However, people will worry so much that they can manifest their own heart attack and it does happen often.

We arrived home in San Diego at 3:00am and I was abducted from my house that morning. Heidi was sleeping over at my place, even sleeping on the floor in the same room I was in, but again she was not taken. I believe now that she could have been a handler.

That night I was taken in a jeep to a waiting helicopter. I started to wake up when I saw the helicopter and I began struggling. I heard someone say, "Sedate the bitch," and I was given a shot in the arm. I was taken to what I think was a base and told to put on fatigues, which were very heavy and scratchy. I was then ordered to run. I ran with several other soldiers in full gear, including an M16 rifle. We ran through caves and tunnels, all over the underground bases. They treated me as if I was a soldier. I woke up exhausted in my bed with huge bruises on my legs. I had woken up often with such bruises and scratches.

I finally ended my friendship with this woman because she always seemed to be around when I was taken. That and the fact that her father was a colonel in the Navy and she was a spoiled rich girl who spent all her time running around and never even worked. I wondered how she made her money, since she always seemed to have plenty of it. A handler has many duties but an important one is they are supposed to make sure you are in the correct place. They also keep you controlled through possibly drugging you. Their job is to keep a very close eye on you and usually it is a friend, boyfriend, husband and other kinds of relatives. I have had many boyfriend handlers, two husband handlers and few female friend handlers such as Heidi. I guess that's why right now I do not date and I keep to myself. Someday I'd like to learn how to trust again.

THE D.U.M.B.S

Much of my childhood and my most of my adult life up to age 40 has huge blank areas, due to severe trauma-based mind control perpetrated by my father and other men. My feelings about my father are very mixed but after some time, and a lot of therapy, I learnt how to forgive him. I feel sorry for him because he was also mind controlled from early childhood to do what he did to me so I can't really hate him, but I also can't really love him. I saw a picture of him at ten years old dressed in a dress, with ringlets, more than likely part of ritual and mind control programming. I also heard from my father himself of horrific beatings he was given all through his life, and on one occasion my great uncle witnessed the blood on his clothes and his bleeding back when he ran away to his uncle's (my great uncle's) house. I will talk more about him in the next volume. I will also write about the missing period between January 1967 and August 1967, 8 months of missing time which included a marriage of which I had no idea. I will also get into another eight months of missing time between 1968 and 1969, but for now I will share more recent experiences.

Early in 1990 I was living in Las Vegas, NV, with my husband and my two sons. Trying to live a normal life was hard because of all the abductions my family was having. I have one specific memory of waking up in an elevator. I saw other people in it too. There were people on each side of me and everyone was in a catatonic state. There was a soldier at the front, right next to the door, with a machine gun.

It was kind of funny because there were several people in front of me in various kinds of clothing: some had clothes on, some wore pajamas, some were just in their underwear, and there were some who had no clothes on at all. I think this was due to the different time zones people were taken from. The elevator stopped and I remember it opening, but it opened differently to a regular elevator as the doors opened in a zigzag motion. We were shuffled out the door and as I was being moved off towards the left there was a kind of hold up from the people in front, who were being moved towards the right of me.

I looked at them and saw my 14-year-old son being taken by the military men to a group of 6 ft tall beige gray aliens with long skinny arms and pale skin. Seeing my son taken away and not even being able to move or help him was so frightening to me. I was thinking, "OMG, will I ever see him again?" I was ushered over to a group of black uniformed military and then taken for interrogation. They took me into a small room with a mirrored glass and a table like the ones you see in the doctor's office. I only have a few memories of this event, but I know that it was abusive because I woke up in my bed the next day with bruises on my inner thighs. I have flashes of being raped by these men. The men in the black uniforms took me into a small room with a one way glass. I can't remember anything else after that.

One other night I was taken to the same small room with gray walls for what I later found out to be interrogation. During this interrogation, men in black uniforms and a man in a white lab coat were asking me where the bases were. "Where is his base?" they demanded. I knew they were talking about my reptilian friend Iyano, who has told me that they have been at war with the reptilians underground on Earth for millennia.

They asked me, "Where's the alien space craft?" I was steadfast in saying, "I don't know what you're talking about." They again questioned me about the ship, saying, "I know the ship has landed here. Where is the ship?" Again, I said, "I have no idea what you're talking about." The man in a lab coat came in and they forced something down my throat.

It was a vial of thick greenish, yellow liquid and it felt slimy as it went down my throat. It didn't take long for me to understand what it was. I felt it was a drug of some kind, because of the way it made me feel. Everything was blurry and moving and I could only see a few feet in any direction. I saw three men in uniform standing around me and then a reptilian walked into the room.

Chitahurri (who was the same type of reptilian I saw in 1965)

It was the same kind of reptilian I had seen in 1965. I call them the Chutukari. I'm not sure where I heard that name, but it must have been telepathically. I have since found out that there are reptilians seen in Africa. Credo Mutwah, an African medicine man, talks about the Chitahurri, saying that if the Chitahurri eat the meat of humans they become very high. This is an interesting point considering the ritual that I experienced in 1965, and later instances in my life, because the Draconians like to use humans in rituals and drink their blood because its makes them high. I was thinking these might be the same ones.

The reptilian bent down and looked into my eyes and I was not able to close them. I know that the reptilian used some type of mind manipulation, like a Vulcan mind meld on me, as in Star Trek. He was dark green, about 7 ft tall, and I believe he was of the same species I had seen many times before in the underground bases. This time though, when he looked into my eyes, I felt like things were being pulled out of my brain. It was like he was siphoning off my memories or sifting through them. I had images appear in my head. I would access a picture and then it seemed to be gone, then another and another.

I felt as though he was stealing my memories. I thought, "He's trying to find out about my friends. I can't think about my alien friends and my team. I can't." But at that moment I heard a very strong loving voice in my head from my dear friend Iyano saying, "Do not worry, you will not give the base location up." I thought to myself, "Oh my God! I can't think of the base, I can't think of the base." I tried to think of anything else but that was the only image coming up in my head. I had to think of something else, but once again his voice came through, saying, "Do not worry, you will not tell our location."

To be honest with you, I was really out of my mind from the drugs and I don't remember if he got things out of my mind or not. I have a feeling that he did, but I know I have an ocular implant (eye implant) that connects me to Iyano's group, and this connection was very strong and powerful. Perhaps this implant may have been strong enough to override their interrogation techniques. I truly hoped so because there was a period of time that I did not see Iyano, and I worried that his base had been compromised.

MY CONTACT WITH IYANO

Thankfully however, I did see him a few weeks later. He told me that they had to make some adjustments to their base and location, but they had evacuated the area by the time the attack occurred. Thank goodness he made it out. He said they were aware of the behaviors of other reptoids, since they have been at war with them for millennia.

I want to explain that all communications with Iyano or his team have been telepathic. Whenever they communicated with me it was through whole thought forms, like sentence pictures.

I learned so much from my 20 year connection with Iyano and the rest of his Federation. I had my first contact with Iyano in Las Vegas in 1989. All I had known for so many years was negative reptilians. I would have a positive ET experience and then within hours or a few days I would have a visit from grays who in turn would take me to the reptilians or the black ops military. I believe that these grays were just clones since they had no emotion and not even really an energy so they could have even been non-biological units.

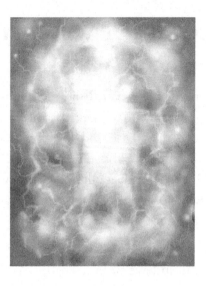

The first time I was with Iyano

One night my husband was out of town for his job, which usually was not good for my kids and me because he was a long haul truck driver and gone all the time. This night however, everything changed. Instead of the usual abduction I had my first encounter with a positive reptilian. There in the darkness of my bedroom he appeared, a glowing silhouette of light. I couldn't completely make out his features because he was wearing some kind of a robe but the colors were magnificent, beautiful different colors in a vortex of energy.

The other times he came to me through the same energy vortex. He would take me aboard a ship and teach me. I received many downloads at that time and I believe that I was in some kind of training. I would hear different dialects and different languages. I even saw dialects and languages on virtual, almost holographic, screens. I never remembered seeing others on the ship except him, the other reptilians, and only one other type of grays, so mostly I just felt that I would never be harmed. I was always treated with unconditional loving energy by Iyano and all others of his group.

One night after months and months of visits from him I awoke and saw a tall handsome blonde human man. I think that is what my mind could handle since I've always been afraid of reptiles. I knew it was Iyano because I recognized his energy, but I knew this wasn't really what he looked like. I said to him, "You are something else, what do you really look like?" He said, "Are you sure you are ready to see me as I am?" I said "Yes." He said again, "Are you absolutely sure you want to see me as I really am? Are you sure you're ready?" I said "Yes."

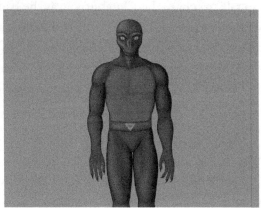

There stood a 7.5 ft or more regal reptilian being. I was frightened at first, but I felt kindness and even a loving energy from him. I felt no fear, only love. He had a light avocado greenish color to his scales, and he had piercing but kind, beautiful yellow eyes. His body structure was very muscular and he had some type of armor on his chest, however I think it was part of his body as it was organic, and it reminded me of a turtle shell on his front chest. He wore a belt on his waist and two bands around his wrist. I believe the bands were for communication. The belt had a kind of triangle buckle that pointed down, and it had a symbol in the middle. He wore a black cloak but I could see his hands and I only saw four fingers with long claw like nails. I was frightened at first but I felt the unconditional love that was coming from him. Again I felt no fear, only love. This was such a different energy and feeling compared to the other reptilian encounters I have had before with the reptilians from the underground bases. When I did hear him talk, to chase the Chitahurri away, he had a low guttural growl. Most of the time all he had to do was look at them and they would leave. He became my protector. He would always come to me in an energy vortex and then we would leave through this same vortex gate. I think this vortex is like a Merkabah for them to travel in.

After many other visits, he told me what his name was. It was absolutely impossible for me to say so he shortened it to Iyano, at least, that is what I heard in my head. He told me he was something like an ambassador and his highly involved race had been at war with the service-to-self reptilians and tall grays, the group that lives under the earth. He said that his species is service-to-others and they do not wish to harm anyone, but they had been at war with this other reptilian and tall gray group for millennia. He never did tell me where he was from but it must have been off planet because they arrived in ships and I only saw the ship.

Iyano visited me physically for many years throughout this period of my life until 2001. I do not remember any physical contact with Iyano since.

The Chitahurri tried once again to get back in through technology and my computer, like they had before, but he stopped them again. He is still with me to this day and I believe he is still protecting me and always will, as I have been told.

I have learned so much from my life experiences that I would never change these experiences and what I learned from them. I learned so much from Iyano and the Federation. We truly are spiritual beings living a human life. I guess I was taking care of some karma from past lifetimes and learning more about being a human. Because of all my experiences, I understand and have empathy and compassion for so many who have experienced the same things.

The Galactic Federation of Light was founded over 4.5 million years ago to prevent inter-dimensional dark forces from dominating and exploiting this galaxy. At present there are just over 200,000 member star nations, confederations and unions. Approximately 40%

are humanoids and the rest are varied forms of sentient beings. Most members of the Galactic Federation are fully conscious beings. I believe that we, as starseeds, are from these federations and are here to help Earth.

These experiences with Iyano and others like him taught me that you can't judge an ET (alien) by how they look. Just because they look scary and maybe ugly from human standards does not mean they are evil, and just because they look human and are beautiful does not mean they are from the light. We must be discerning at all times. There is good and bad in all races, including the human race. As above, so below.

Iyano as he appeared to me in 1989

I am going to talk briefly about implants. I feel the ocular implant that Iyano's people put in me was to help me. My health is perfect. I look younger than I am and they know where I am so they can protect me. Iyano does protect me to this day. That is what was helping me in the interrogation when the reptilian was trying to find where Iyano's base was.

Implants are energetic devices that can be inserted into the physical body or vibrationally held in the 4D etheric interface with the body. These devices are meant to control behavior or block normal flows of energy through the body of the individual.

Some implants can be of a positive nature, and these would have been put into the etheric or physical body as per agreements made with benevolent ETs. Some are like software added to be able to communicate.

Many starseeds are implanted with these positive devices. These are mostly of an etheric nature and would be used for healing, locating, and monitoring the spiritual awakening of the individual. I have multiple implants, just one that I know of from Iyano's group (the ocular implant on my left side), as well as other implants from different ET groups.

There are some methods to remove implants (whether they are physical or etheric). The ones that we want to remove are the negative ones. They can be located anywhere on the body, but usually are somewhere in the head area as this is the most effective way to control someone's thought processes. If they are located in organs and other areas of the body, they are usually used to control someone's health and stop them from being able to connect with their higher selves, thus potentially thwarting ascension.

THE THREAT

Later in 1999 I was working with a fellow MILAB abductee and researcher, Melinda Leslie. We were planning a tell all book and had been interviewing MILAB abductees, both civilian and military. The following are all the things the black ops did to me that finally caused me quit my research into Mk-Ultra, ritual abuse, targeted individuals, and super soldiers. It started with many anonymous calls telling me to quit, throughout 1999 and 2000. I believe the first warning was definitely related to the threats I had received.

On June 26, 2000 at around 12.00am on a very foggy night, I was involved in a very strange car accident with Melinda. I was driving my car on Rancho Santa Fe Road just outside Carlsbad, CA, when a bright light blinded me, causing me to slam into the side of a hill. I don't know what kind of car could have made such a bright light to blind me, since we had seen no cars on the road. My only real option was to hit the hill, the alternative being the edge of a pretty high cliff, which could have meant death. The air bags deployed so we were only slightly injured. Melinda sustained a bump on the knee and I wasn't hurt at all, except for some burns from the air bags deploying.

The next morning at work somebody pointed out that my license plate was missing so I went back to see if I could find it on the side of the hill. I took my keys and started walking beside the road up the hill. A car went past me and soon after I saw it come speeding back towards me, followed by a pickup truck.

I found my license plate on the side of the hill and started back down the road. When I got close to my car I could see something glistening on the ground, and I saw that my window had been broken on the passenger side. Upon opening the door I saw that my purse was gone. I was shocked, and thought, OMG! Who would do such a thing? I felt pretty helpless. My purse had my phone and all my IDs in it. I didn't know what to do. I didn't want to leave the scene and no one else had stopped, since it wasn't a busy road.

However, what I didn't realize was that there had been an eye witness to the event. The man driving the pickup truck pulled up and came over excitedly. He proceeded to tell me he had seen the whole thing. He told me how a truck had pulled out in front of him so quickly that he had to hit the brakes hard so that he wouldn't hit it. He saw my broken window and starting following the truck. When he pulled up alongside it he saw a man wrapping up his bleeding arm with a rag of some kind. He took a mental picture of the man and fell back behind him, making a note of his license number, make and model. Then he returned to help me. He had called the police because they showed up right after the incident.

Even though there was an eye witness and they caught the guy a few days later, none of my belongings were returned to me. My purse and everything in it was gone. I went to court when the truck driver was being arraigned. The thief made a statement for the judge's acquisition. He admitted that he was an addict and said he was sorry he had broken into my car and stolen my purse. The judge asked, "Where are her purse and belongings?" The thief replied that he had sold my driver's license, social security card, credit cards and check book on the black market and had thrown my purse into a garbage can.

He plead guilty and was sentenced. The most terrible thing about this incident was that, before I could get all of my accounts closed, I had charges and bounced checks all over the city. I was a victim of identity theft and it caused so many problems with my credit for several years afterward.

I experienced a lot of harassment from certain people but I believe it was driven by the black ops and power elite. It was very obvious that they were following me and their vehicles were often parked close to my home. I was also sure they tapped my phone calls. Often during my conversations with other people they would come on the line, make snide remarks, and then hang up. Things would go missing in my house and I would find my mail had been tampered with, as well as my emails.

Melinda and I often had interviews with men and women for the book we were writing. In late 2000 we were still researching and interviewing lots of retired military and special forces personnel. I conducted quite a few interviews in my home so I didn't think anything of it when someone contacted me and said that he had been in the military in special forces and that he had much to tell me, so I made an appointment for him to come to my house the next day.

He arrived at my home as scheduled and I opened the door and invited him in. He sat on the couch, and after introductions we started the interview. Initially there were no issues with this person, who was a large black man weighing about 250 pounds. As I interviewed him he seemed as if he was becoming very agitated, and all of a sudden he starting acting really crazy. He said, "You seem like a nice lady and I feel bad for you because they want you dead, since you won't shut up!" He told me, "I was sent to kill you. I'm just following orders from the major, he's my commanding officer." I could hardly believe what I was hearing, as this man was sitting there on my couch saying all this to me.

I had to do some really quick thinking since he now seemed unstable and crazy. I thought I would be able to bluff him, so this is what I did: in the most powerful and demanding voice I could muster, I stood up and paced back and forth in front of him and told him, "I also have a commander and he is a colonel. My commander is above your major in rank and my commander's orders are more important than your major's." I told him he had to go back and check with his major to see which orders to follow, that all orders are to be canceled by my superior officer, the colonel.

And, thank God, it worked. I had confused him enough to leave. Once he was gone and out of sight, I ran and jumped in my car, went to the police station and reported the incident. The police made a report and showed me some mug shots and I finally saw him and pointed him out. The police officer told me that he was on parole from prison for sexual offenses, though he could not tell me exactly what type. He told me the next step. I took the report to the court house and got a restraining order against him. I returned home with high hopes they would catch him and this would be over.

However, he came back to my house the next evening and pounded on my door, and since my car was in the garage, out of view, I hoped he would think I was not home. I quickly and quietly went to my bedroom and called the police. I hid in my bedroom for what seemed like forever, waiting for him to go away. I thought he might have left when he heard sirens. The police came and took my statement and told me not to worry, that they had his name and description and knew where he worked. They reassured me, saying, "Don't worry, we will get him." A few days later the police called me and told me I would not have to worry about him anymore as he had violated his parole and had been sent back to prison.

There are many times where I would meet complete strangers and they would say things to me like, "Aren't you worried that they'll come after you?" Even in dating life I had odd warnings. The men I met and dated always seemed to be in the Navy or other military branches, and on occasion, I think I might have even turned one of their special forces guys into being my friend. He also said, "Aren't you worried about messing around with such things? I like you and you really need to get out of this. You know I don't want you hurt, but you're messing with some pretty powerful people out there." Despite this, I continued on my project.

THE THREAT ACTED OUT

The next physical warning I had was on August 20, 2000. Melinda had stayed over at my condo in La Costa, CA, because we were working on a book and we were going to have an interview on the Art Bell, Dream Land radio show with Mike Siegel. The interview was going very well until all of a sudden I was asked, "Have you ever seen different looking aliens besides the grays in the underground bases?" I started to share my experience about the reptilian when the call was cut off. Melinda's phone did not disconnect so she continued the interview.

It took a good 20 minutes for me to get back on the phone, and by then the interview was almost over. We didn't really think too much of it, though I thought it was kind of odd that I wasn't able to speak about reptilians on the radio.

We worked on our research the next day and that night and as it was so late Melinda stayed another night. We woke up the next morning and noticed that my coffee table had been broken. Melinda had been sleeping on the couch and did not remember falling on the coffee table or breaking it. It was very odd because there had to be a reason for it being broken. Melinda then had to go back home to Laguna Hills.

I really had an uncomfortable and uneasy

feeling, so I went and had a regression done. I found out later that Melinda too had the same very uneasy feeling about that night but we didn't know why. It was odd that we both had the same very creepy feelings since she was over in Laguna Hills and I was some 60 miles away in La Costa. We had various conversations about how something was wrong, but we couldn't remember anything. We both decided to investigate things further through hypnosis.

She did hers with her therapist in Laguna and I did mine with my therapist here. In regression we both found out about the night. We both saw a group of military black ops, in black uniforms and night vision goggles. They had come into my condo and abducted us. I recounted how I had been taken out of my bed by two men in night vision goggles and dark uniforms.

I was feeling very drugged and could not walk. The men held each arm and I was virtually carried down the stairs to a waiting van.

Melinda found from her hypnosis that she'd had a very similar experience. She had been woken up by them when they were picking her up off the sofa. She felt drugged and dizzy and had fallen onto my coffee table, breaking it. They had put us in the van feet to head so if we woke up we couldn't talk. I also feel they did it that way to add to our confusion, so we would not know where they had taken us.

The ride in the van was very hard. I kept waking

up and falling back to sleep but Melinda remembers more than I do. The next thing I remember is the van coming to a stop. I saw a light coming through the window of the front passenger side seat, and then I was dragged out of the van and taken into a building.

To me it looked like an airplane hanger. We were both taken to different rooms and interrogated by humans in dark uniforms. The room I was in seemed to be dimly lit, almost dark, but there was a very bright light on me that blinded me, so I could not make out the faces of the other people in the room. I could see a man in uniform standing at the door with a large weapon that appeared to be a machine gun. I sat up and I was on a table, the kind you see in a doctor's office, but metal.

There was a man in uniform. I feel he was an officer. He said to me, "You stupid bitch, we have told you to stop talking. You might think this is your mission but it is over now. You will stop writing the book and stop lectures and never talk about it again. Go back home, find a husband and get married, forget about all of this because **it's not going to bring you any happiness**." These are the same words that had been said to me before when I was interrogated and threatened, and they were said to me again during another threat, later that year. I believe them to be trigger words, so when I hear them they are supposed to cause me to act a certain way, triggering an internal program to do what they will me to.

He went on to say, "To show you how serious this is, I want you to meet someone else." Then through the door and out of the darkness came a Draconian. He was close to 7 or 8 ft tall with light greenish gold, very scaly looking skin. He had what appeared to be skin protruding at his shoulders over his back that could have been wings, or what was left of them. He had a long tail that swished back and forth when he walked over to me. He bent down and stared deep into my eyes. This seemed to be similar to other mind meld techniques that I had experienced with reptilians in the underground bases, but this was very different because he put a horrific vision into my head that terrified me.

The vision in my head was of my family, my children and grandchild all being dismembered. I watched in horror as black uniformed Ninja soldiers with long swords chopped them up in front of my eyes. I stood there, helpless to stop them, and it the most horrible sight I had ever seen. However, there was one thing that wasn't right. I could not hear anything, no screams, no noise came from this horrible vision I was experiencing. I thought to myself, this is not real, and I remember saying, "Is this real or Memorex?" At that moment I came out of this hypnotic state.

I broke his trance. I don't remember him leaving. I'm not even sure that there really was a Draconian in the room at all. Was it possible I had been hypnotized by humans and there was no Draconian ever there? It's possible that a human gave me a hypnotic suggestion to make me see the draconian and make me see this whole scenario.

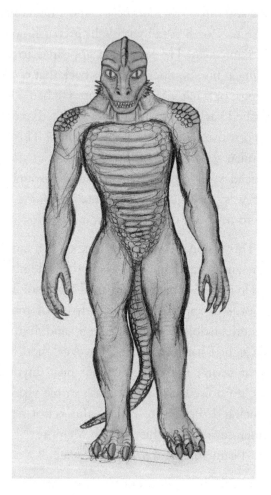

The Draconian I saw from the base during my and Melinda's abduction

Description of Melinda's Draconian from the base

Melinda remembered in her regression that she had a very similar interrogation, also with a Draconian. This was the first time she had ever seen a reptilian (Draconian). She told me he put an image in her mind of him attacking her, raping her and dismembering her.

I don't know if it was just how we pictured and described it or if there were two of them, or was it even real?! The odd thing was, her Draconian and my Draconian were similar but our descriptions to the artist differed somewhat. Our descriptions to the artist had different colors and some other differences. David Chace is a very talented forensic artist and he did both pictures for us, but years apart. David is the best at drawing reptilian aliens. He has drawn many pictures for me, some of which are in my books.

Melinda and I talked briefly over the phone about our individual regressions. Our stories corroborated each other. We decided we would talk about our experiences later because they had been so upsetting to both of us. We just weren't ready to relive it again.

What is the Evidence for My Experiences?

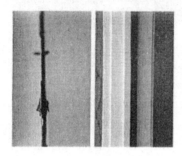

Damage to door frame from forced-entry into home from one of Melinda's experiences. Picture on left shows how wood frame was forcefully pulled apart at seam. Picture on right is of undamaged section to show how same seam should appear.

What is the Evidence for My Experiences?

Damage to door frame and foam weather-stripping from forced-entry into home during one of Melinda's experiences. Picture on left shows damage around door deadbolt area and on right shows damage around door lock including a chunk out of wood.

I took pictures of door jams and the break in (pictured above). We didn't talk to each other about the real details of that night until 16 years later. We were interviewed on the Aquarian radio show by Dr. Sasha and Janet Lessin in June 2016. I know these abductors wanted me to know that they could come into my house to take me anytime and that they could do whatever they wanted to me. We however, did not quit our research and continued interviewing people for our book.

In late 2000, Melinda and I attended a conference just after the abduction in San Diego. Melinda and I were talking with Dr. John Mack and Richard Hoagland about our research, about the book, and about all the problems that we had both had because of our research for the book. They both told us that this was a very important book and that we needed to finish it. "You need to write this, it will help so many people," they said, so we decided that there was nothing that was going to stop us. We continued our research and interviewed more of retired military and special forces personnel for our book, since that seemed to be where the answers were.

THE MAN IN THE COBRA

I talked to my kids and told them what the two researchers had said. I also told them about the threats I had received. I didn't want to frighten them, but I did also tell them about the incident with the Draconian on the base. They said, "Mom, this is important and you need to keep going with your research. We can take care of ourselves."

In late November, 2000, I got a call from a man who said he had been in the special forces. He said he had some really good information for me. I had learned my lesson from the previous dangerous encounter so from then on I would only do interviews in a public place, until I got to know them and find out if they were safe. I was to meet him in a restaurant bar.

He showed up in a green flight jacket with a Lt. Colonel emblem on the pocket. The first words out of his mouth were, "So how is that cute little granddaughter of yours in _____ Nevada? She is 3 now, isn't she?" I knew I was in trouble. How did he know I had a granddaughter in _____ Nevada? I said, "How would you know I have a granddaughter?" He said, "We know everything about you and your little family. We know your granddaughter's age, your son's age, where they work, we know their routines and everything about them. They find people's bones in the desert all the time. You think you're so smart little lady but you're not. You need to forget about this. The people are not ready to hear what you have to say."

I replied that they have a right to know. He said, "What would happen if the masses knew that the aliens were real and that they could come and go as they chose and could abduct anyone they wanted to, without us being able to do anything to stop them? The people would be terrified. It would cause panic and cause everything to fail. The world is just not ready to hear this. Little girl you need to stop what you're doing and go find a man, get married and forget about all of this, because **this is not going to bring you any happiness**." Again, here was the phrase I had heard several times before.

He then got up from the table and left. I followed him out the door to see what kind of vehicle he was in. He saw I had followed him. I guess that pissed him off because he proceeded to scream at me in the parking lot, saying that it would be harmful to my family if I continued on the path I was on. He said, "It would be a shame if something happened to you or your family. Remember, there is a big desert out there." As he was getting into the car he screamed, "Keep your f-----ing mouth shut." A couple in the parking lot heard him screaming and asked if I was okay, because they could see how shaken up I was. He saw them and got into his shiny new black Cobra and sped away.

On December 23, I was driving home on Interstate 15 for the holidays. I was driving middle lane at 72 mph with my cruise control on when a white van passed in the fast lane and disappeared out of sight. Shortly after that I came up on a line of tractor trailers in the slow right lane. Then, all of a sudden, the white van that had passed me earlier pulled out from between two trucks and forced me off the road. I remember thinking that I was going to die this time. My car went out of control, moving across the median and into the path of oncoming traffic but, amazingly, I was able to get it under control enough to return to my side of the median. Then, incredibly, a Joshua cactus tree was in front of me and everything appeared to be moving in slow motion as I came to a very soft landing on the cactus tree. Someone told me once that if you're about to die and you resolve yourself to it, your angels/ETs will help you to survive. That is how this experience felt to me. I went back many times after the event and could not find the Joshua tree. I feel it was truly a miracle.

A trucker and his wife stopped to help me. He said they had seen the whole thing and could not figure out what the white van was doing in their lane in the first place. He said it looked like it was intentional.

The trucker said to me, "That was a fine piece of driving, keeping that fire-bird from flipping over." He said he radioed ahead to other truckers to get the license plate of the van, and that he had called 911 for me. The damage to my car was not too bad, just that the bumper was hanging off and there were dents on the front hood. It was a miracle that the cactus tree was there, because the road is a stretch road where there are very few cacti. It's as if someone put it there for me to hit and stop my car. It saved my life most likely. Incredibly, I was unharmed, even though I had my T Top open on my Firebird and branches from the cactus were in my backseat. I had very few scratches, my airbags had not deployed and I could still drive my car. I did call my son and he came out and helped me by pulling off the bumper so I could drive home. He followed me home to make sure I got to his house safely.

I spent the holiday with my family. I knew this time they were serious, so I told my family that I had decided I was getting out before something happened to them. I told them I was going to go back and close my group and turn over all my interview tapes, interview notes, written material and all pictures and other research to my research partner Melinda Leslie.

When I got back to San Diego I took my car into the shop for repairs and got my rental car. I don't usually get the extra insurance but for some reason I did this time.

I met with Melinda. Well, needless to say I turned everything over to her, having told her everything that had happened to me in the last 2 weeks. I wished her luck and she wished me luck.

Next I was going to a friend's house to give him all of my books. While I was driving there, an SUV blew through the red light and hit me broadside, spinning my car around. The guy who jumped out of the SUV was a large man with a military buzz haircut. He screamed at me, saying it was my fault. He said, "You will have to take the blame." He kept repeating, "It's your fault, it's your fault." I knew something was fishy. Just then two people walking down a hill heard him yell at me. They came over to my car and said they would be my witnesses. The police arrived and did an investigation and talked with the eyewitness, then issued him a citation. Once again, my angels were with me. I was not hurt but my rental car was un-drivable.

I stayed out of everything from that day on for almost 9 years. I closed my groups, never attending anything else. I got away from it all. I never talked to any of my friends or my colleagues in the research field. I closed that part of my life. I tried to have a normal life but in my heart I was always wondering, what if I had never left? We could have finished the book. However, I decided I needed to go on with my life. I continued on with my job working for a home builder in my field as an executive administrator, just living life because I was happy to be alive. I thought this was last of it.

THE SEXUAL ASSAULT

A year later, at the end of 2002, I was trying to get on with my life and meet someone for a relationship. I met a guy on a dating site. We set up to meet at a golf driving course. As was my custom I only met men in a public place and only in the daytime. When I got there he was drinking a cup of coffee. He asked if I would like one. He went to the snack area and brought the coffee out to me on the driving range.

That was the last thing I remembered until I briefly woke up in the woods while he was raping me. Because of the drugs he had given me I could only scream on the inside. I could not fight him off or run because I was unable to control my body, or even move it.

The next thing I remember was waking up in my car behind the wheel. He must have given me a lot of drugs because I could not remember what happened to me until late that night. I was in a fog all day. I called my friend and she met me at a restaurant, and I felt very strange but had no memory. As we talked I was having flashbacks about the attack. I starting getting more flashes and pieced together my memories of what occurred. Around 9pm we left and she took me to the police station.

After making a full report to the police, the police told me he had probably given me Ketamine Rohypnol or "roofies" (the date rape drug). The management (CIA) have used it within their mind control system. It is the most known of amnesia drugs. Rohypnol has been used because it renders its victims incapable of resisting, giving it the reputation of the "date rape" drug.

When I gave them the location of the attack they looked at each other and said, "We are sorry, but this is not our jurisdiction." It had happened on the border of Carlsbad and they were Oceanside Police. They said they were very sorry but I had to go to the Carlsbad Police Department. I could not go through anything else that night. I went home, showered and cried. I had to work the next day, and that morning I tried to function but I broke down and told my boss what had happened to me. He sent one of the other secretaries with me to the police station. The policeman at Carlsbad Police Department was mean, cold and accusatory with me. He was an older man and he said, "If you go on dating sites you had better expect to meet some perverts. You're asking for trouble. It's your own fault." I left after filing a report, as he had been cruel and heartless and no help to me. He also said they did not have a rape kit at the station and he told me it was probably too late anyway.

He did give me the rape crisis information

and I later went to the talk with the rape counselors. They were very nice and gave me good advice on how to proceed.

I was called back by a detective a few days later. He told me I could press charges and go to court but since it was a date rape it was just his word against mine that it ever happened. They said he had no priors and had never been arrested, so he appeared to be a solid citizen. I asked for his name so I could get him checked out myself but the police said they couldn't give me his name. I felt that was just so wrong. He said that if I chose to go ahead with this and go to court, when I got on the stand, it could get very ugly for me. I decided not to pursue it any longer, even though my rape counselor told me I should. I am not sure if the government sent the rapist after me but I have always wondered. I went through extensive therapy and learned to deal with what he did to me. This was an awful thing to happen but I've had much worse done to me, like what had happened to me during my missing times for many years.

It's difficult to get it all in chronological order, so for this reason I have periods of missing time in my life, from childhood on to about age 35. This is when I started to remember my life, a process that has continued to this day. I still have big gaps in memory, with not much of anything between 1965 and 1985. I don't even remember things like my graduation, wedding, or either of my sons' births or birthdays.

Memories have surfaced, ranging from very minor memories to very severe memories including body memory of the physical trauma that I was put through in order to ingrain programming in me. I was in Mk-Ultra and Monarch programs, and in Project Talent. There was sex slavery, ritualistic abuse, and other trauma-based torture methods. I have done a lot of work on both my missing periods of time, each 7 - 9 months through 1968 to 1970. I have a wedding and marriage I don't remember, but those memories are coming back too. I know what happened to me was so terrible and the rape brought it all back. Believe me when I say that what happened to me in those missing periods of my life was much worse than the rape.

I will write about my own MK-Ultra Programming from childhood to adulthood. MK-Ultra is a mind control program developed by the CIA, and tested on the military, civilians, men, women, even children and babies. These projects started in the 40s and continue to this day. There are many different projects under the umbrella of MK-Ultra. These programs use combinations of hypnosis, drugs, and psychosurgery to create agents out of their victims, along with severe torture intended to fracture and compartmentalize the mind and ensure compliance. LSD, Ketamine, Psilocybin, lobotomies, and electroshock are among the many drugs and surgeries that are used and experimented with, for both programming and memory wipes. Agents only know what they're programmed to know and even then their memories tend to be erased once the missions are complete.

Hypnosis was used to bury my memories so I am using hypnosis to unbury them. It is working! In future volumes I will talk about my positive ET experiences, hybrid children and my starseed galactic family. In my next book, 'They Weren't Butterflies - A Monarch Survivor's Story', I will recount my missing years of my life, starting with my childhood programing.

I have enclosed some characteristics of a MILAB and Mk-Ultra experiencers. Please take some time and answer these questions. They will give your insight to your own experiences.

The End of Volume 1

QUESTIONNAIRE

MK-Ultra, Super Soldier, Secret Space Program, Monarch, Montauk, and Ritual Abuse Questionnaire

This list is not an absolute means of determining if you have had these types of experiences, and if you have there may be <u>many</u> other explanations for these occurrences. If many of these questions apply to you, please see a qualified researcher or therapist. You may email ladene99@yahoo.com if you desire more information or wish to share your results. No name is necessary; this is an anonymous questionnaire.

There are two types of MILAB abductions, the first is to be taken into DUMBs for questioning about your ET experiences. The other type of MILAB and MK-Ultra abduction is to interrogate you and to program you to be a unwitting spy against the ETs, like a double agent with implants from both the ET and the MK-Ultra groups. It is not uncommon to have vague memories of these experiences, and these memories can come back to you through your dreams or flashbacks. Which one, if either, applies to you?

1. Do you have psi (psychic) abilities? For example, do you astral travel (OBE), remote view, perform psychokinesis (move matter with your mind), or do you have mediumship and telepathy (mind reading) abilities?

2.   Do you have memories of waking up from sleep as a child, or an adult one day, feeling like you lost time and having trouble remembering things you should know? Do you have no memories of some of your childhood? Or perhaps flashes of another possible life?

3.   Have you had dreams of being locked into a small box or coffin?

4.   As a child or adult, have you ever seen or been put in tanks of liquid?

5.   Do you have dreams of having friends tortured or killed in front of you?

6.   Have you ever seen human military space vehicles or spacecraft? Did you travel in any?

7.   Have you had dreams that you were put in cages? Or dreams that you saw others in cages?

8.   Have you had dreams that you were put in tiny dark rooms, almost like a closet with just a cot?

9.   Have you had dreams of being a military soldier? Or dreams of being in uniforms running and training with a military guns and packs on your back?

10. Have you ever seen human uniforms (especially military) during your abductions? If so, what insignias were on them?

11. Have you been taken to an underground facility or off this planet by aliens or by humans?

12. Have you had any form of intimidation from

humans in your abduction memories? For example, verbal warnings, threats to you or your family's life or safety, physical abuse, or have you been beaten-up or roughed-up?

13. During an abduction, have human doctors performed any medical procedures?

14. As a child, have you been taken out of school and tested?

15. Do you have large spans of days, weeks, months, or even years you don't remember?

16. Have you been in a small grey room that has a mirror? Did you feel watched?

17. Do you have dreams or memories of being tortured with spiders and snakes, and/or snakes used in rituals?

18. Have people ever interrogated and tortured you with electric shock? Have you had dreams of apparatus or bands put on your head for electric shock.

19. Have you been strapped in a trip chair (much like a dentist chair) and felt like you have traveled through time, whether past or future?

20. Do you know the term 'pleasure versus pain' and what it means?

21. In relation to your abductions, have you had any forms of the following harassment: black helicopters, telephone interruption/noises, calls at odd hours of the night, mail tampered with or missing, email tampered

with, being followed, being outright approached, or run-ins or confrontations with military or government types?

22. Have you been given scopolamine or other truth injections to cause you to do things beyond your will, and then had amnesia?

23. Have you had cattle prods or other shock wands used on you to force you to comply?

24. Have you seen or used human military weapons with alien technology during an abduction?

25. Have you had dreams of being used as a beta sex slave?

26. Have you had dreams or memories of witnessing or being used in ritual sacrifices or sexual rituals?

27. Do you feel you've been 'remote influenced' (where your thoughts are not your own) to cause harm to yourself or to harm someone else?

28. Do you currently, or have you ever, lived near or on a military base or facility?

29. Have you been used as a courier or messenger, with a photographic memory?

30. Have you ever had experiences with Men-In-Black?

31. Have you been abducted by military personnel without any aliens being present?

32. Did the aliens or the military instruct you in their technology or show you how it works? For example,

have you seen propulsion systems? Or have you flown, navigated or worked the controls in a ship?

33. Have you had dreams of being put into a dentist-like chair and seeing imagery of unfamiliar places, people, or ETs, and then been questioned?

34. Do you have dreams or memories of being taken onto another planet and spending years there?

35. Do you have dreams or memories of being in a war with aliens where you had no weapons and were used to draw out the enemy?

36. Do you have memories of being in a prison-like facility, or in a small room with just a bed and a sink that was also a toilet?

37. Do you feel flashes and strong memories coming to you often, that make you feel like you are going crazy?

38. Have you had memories of a very unusual ship with a low ceiling and dark or black walls, which reverberated sound?

39. Do you have memories of being an instructor or teacher of small children who you oversaw until they became older?

40. Do you have dreams or memories of time travel? Or of waking up in another time and or planet?

41. Have you been diagnosed with radiation? Or fibromyalgia or other immune diseases?

42. Do you feel like you have navigated or flown ships

and fought wars against aliens?

43. Are you an interface or translator in communicating with extraterrestrials?

44. Do you have flashes and dreams of Nazis?

45. Do you feel your genetics have been used in the Super Soldier Program?

46. Do you speak, write, and understand galactic languages?

47. Do you remember dying and being put in liquid or a machine to bring you back?

48. Do you feel like you are a clone, or that you may have clones of you?

49. Do you have a feeling that many of these things apply to you, but have no memories of them?

50. Do you feel that you don't experience emotions the way others do, concerning loss, grief, pain, and sadness? Do you release your emotions other ways, such as crying at a movie or even on a commercial?

ABOUT THE AUTHOR

Miesha Johnston is a second generational ET experiencer, MILAB and Mk-Ultra survivor. Miesha is a Certified Hypnotherapist. She specializes in Trauma Recovery, ADD & ADHD and Past Live Regression. She works with people who are ET Experiencers, and MILAB, MK-Ultra and Ritual Abuse survivors. She is also a channel and offers private Multi-Dimensional Galactic Light Language Activation Sessions. Miesha facilitates one monthly support group in her private residence in Las Vegas, NV, and three biweekly virtual support groups on the internet through Zoom. Miesha has a Saturday weekly radio show, Starseed Awakening on KCOR Radio, and is the owner and operator of Vector 5 Tours, UFO Night Vision Tours through Air bnb.

Websites: http://starsecdawakening.org

https://www.facebook.com/groups/starseedawakening

www.ufonightwatch.com

Made in the USA
Coppell, TX
16 June 2024